Mental Freak

Tahja Hodge

Presentation by *BookLeaf Publishing*

Web: www.bookleafpub.com

E-mail: info@bookleafpub.com

ISBN: 9789357440073

First edition 2023

To all the Beautiful Souls among the world.
Keep shining your light!!!

ACKNOWLEDGEMENT

I like to thank the lord for one of the many gifts he bestowed upon me, also the numerous colleagues and family members who have continually encouraged me to pursue writing.

My Peak

My desire is peaking
Not wanting anything to hold me back
Push Me
Mentally as well as Physically
Guide me to a state of a higher realm of
intergalactic mind-blowing outer body
intimacies
I have become addicted, to a creation of the
ultimate mind fuck
With intelligent conversations over the seeking
of knowledge and growth spiritually.
Harvest my body from head to toe with truth and
honesty, along with Deep Hard penetration from
your investigator of pleasure

Quick Session

Don't make me back this ass up on you
You better bend me over and own this pussy
from the back
I ain't intending to run
Make me take all that dick
Pussy Dripping
Slowly ease in giving that ass a smack
Let me help, Imma spread these cheeks for ya
Hold on let me get my balance
I don't want it to be slow
I want you to fucking take me
Bound to make this honey cum quick
No stopping till you cum
Wait
Take it out I want a taste

Healing Session

Let me open up
Stick it in, what's my temperature
Can you feel this heat rolling off me
Dig in, I can take it all
I need you to release this pressure
Watch it flow out as you unplug from my
steamed outlet
Release your therapeutic medicine inside
Watch as I ingest the immunity healing potion of
your life giving elixir, made to nurture and calm
my rising storm of temptations

Submission

A night between you and me Investigating and
Exploring
Singing lyrical melodies in each other ears
I open myself up to you
Delve into my library ready to be inspected and
digested for otherworldly knowledge
We have plenty of time to imprint each other
into our minds
Having always something to be learned and
fertilized for future growth
Our senses will be heightened
Engraving the feel of you and taste of you so
much sweeter
Allowing a submission to each other needs

Soul Search

Look into my windows
They are the guide to my soul
They hide nothing and yet leads to everything
that is me
No matter the trials experienced
They will still smile and choose to spread love
Take some time to engage in them
Respect what they are offering, but me mindful
of their boundaries

Ground Me

Grounding is what I need to do, when I have
thoughts about us together
Our love be surpassing multiple planets and
other dimensions
Toxic at best to describe with its exquisite pain
and over sensitive pleasures
Two souls divided crying out for each other
bound in a highly spiritual connection with
endless possibilities.
How can I live without you, even when I never
had the chance to have you
Is this real or creation of a fantasy love
Having unrealistic expectations of the person
you are to me
Questions of my own motives
Why do I feel I have to have you
I may want you but I don't need you
In the end my love for me will always be what I
need and want

Mental Release

I have this feeling of Co-Dependency on you
Every thought of you makes me happy and
heated
I crave the feel of you against and inside me
I don't seem to focus on anything else, and it's
distracting this feeling of obsession and toxicity
from you
The fantasy I have of a connection makes me
feel high and giddy
But the reality of it leaves me with Big
Disappointments and unflattering thoughts.
I know I need to release you from my thoughts
Your residency within them needs to end, but I
can't seem to let you go, even though you don't
belong to me
I don't know and maybe it was meant to be this
way
However it goes I only wish nothing but your
happiness and success

I Need You

I need you
Come look at me
Ready
Legs Open
Hands behind my head
Eyes only for you
A steady drip creating puddles
I need you to take a dive
Explore my little cavern
touch it, taste it, and enter it
Command and demand it for a full cooperation
and release
Take Ownership
Delegate it your special spot for inner peace or
to release your heated aggravations into
I need you
To feed me a piece of your soul that's connected
to your heart as you feast off mine

Rise to the Challenge

Light trickle in the room, highlighting an
exquisite form
Shimmering trail of honey leaving your mouth
watering
Thinking sweet sticky thoughts of entering a
realm of endless possibilities resistant to no
boundaries
There you watch captivated and hypnotized
A slave to heightening passion that's arising
from your core
Helpless to continuing peak of heat that only
your body can generate
Throwing off sparks of friction that draws the
inner dormant animal
The more you watch the more you want
Never on to have things handed to you
To independent to be satisfied with a easy
submission
Charged with the thought of the chase and
conquer, that leaves the game of the hunt more
stimulating and satisfying, Once captured and
Dominated.
Will you continue to watch or rise to the
challenge

Take Me

I want you to take me
Push me up against the wall
Rip off my panties
Raise my leg around your waist
Play with my pussy
Feel the rise of my dimension
The succulent wetness of my parallel universe
Enter my small zone
Untapped by foreign entities
Fresh and Ready to be explored
Take Me
I'm feeling a thirst nothing seems to quench
I crave your touch
You making me cum in your mouth, on your
fingers, and on every inch of you inside of me
It's all mutual feelings
You craving me cum all on you
Me craving you cumming in my mouth, on my
body, and inside my secret avenue of pleasure
that only you have the key to unlock

Intimate Moments

Our lips mesh in a battle of lip sucking
dueling tongues
My hands cradle your head
Your hands draw my hips closer to you
Without the comfort of space you grab my hair
tilting my head slowly, exposing my neck
With a swiping lick you begin to slowly make
little bites down my neck
A hand grab my breast, and pinch a nipple
I trail my nails down your back
Legs wrap around your waist
I take my hand and release your from your
contained pants
Rubbing you against my dewey center
Only for you I wear a skirt rocking no panties
Sleek and Wet
Ready for you to spread me open as you thrust
into me
Slowly building our throbbing ache to a mutual
exhausting climatic finish

I Want You

I want you to penetrate my body as well as my
mind
Stretch my inner core to fit and snuggle your
outer core
Help me lose myself to you as you take control
Breathless moments of intense bonding of
bodily fluids, that draws us closer together
All boundaries broken down reaching sky
heights as we explore subliminal ecstasy
I want you to see me as I show you how much
I'm into you, with self exploration how far I'm
willing to go with you
I want you to show me how much I can get to
you
Let me see how much you need me, as much as I
need you
Imprint yourself onto me
Feed me that hardness only you can bring
I want you to not just make my pussy weep but
release heavy rain down on your electric rod
Giving out steady thick currents of shocks into
my overly sensitive system
I want you to want me just for being me

Sweet Temptation

Thoughts swimming through my mind
I feel a breeze blow between my thighs
Intoxicating and mind-blowing
To touch me you feel the heat of my body
Letting your thoughts intertwine with mine
Smiling dreamily of moments to be
Heart beating rapidly with the race of future
memories
A sting of reality trying to creep in
With a wave of hand I casually brush it away
Wanting to linger in the ecstasy of a possibility
Can't rid myself of these forbidden images
Of something so close but need to remain hidden
The question remains
When can I taste your Sweet Temptation

Sweetest Sin

Watch me as I glide down the center
Taking my time as running sap from a tree
Leaving you hypnotized with my glistening
essence
I'm calling you
Listen closely as I whisper in your ear, what I
want to do to you
Lean real close
Close your eyes
Prepare yourself for the ecstasy you'll find when
your tongue touches my honey
You hear that
That's you moaning from the nectar of my being
Take in more
Let it fill you up as it thickness glides down your
throat
Lost
Is what you become when its aroma hit your
nose
Fine as the most expensive wine and Juicy as the
ripest peach
There's no time for mindless games
Mindless
Is what you become when you dip into my
cherry pie

Just remember it's gonna leave you wanting
Ready to give up your all
To taste a sip of my Sweetest Sin

Playful Looks

I know he's watching me
I can feel the heat of his eyes caressing my skin
He knows I'm watching him
His every movement my eyes follow
He looks back
Our eyes meet as we both look
Like in youthful innocence we glance away
I sense that he likes me, but lack the maturity to
treat me like I should be treated
Despite his unworthiness I find I still like him
To save my heart
I take enjoyment in our continued looks
Whether Intimate
Sometimes Playful
And even Scornful
Finally he approaches me
My mind and body tells me I'm ready
Then he turns around and fucks it up with
Every Word that comes out his mouth

Force of a Woman

Soft n Supple my body feels against you
Sleek
With a glow that shines from the inside out
Confident I stand
A magnet to all sexes
A natural born mother
Nuturer
Giver of the heart
The other half to her mate
Strong enough to support her man
Can hide her insecurities and pains
A person that screams
Lady,
Fighter
And that Freaky trick behind closed doors
A best kept secret
To be treasured and honored
Defender of her family
A true friend
A woman that can't be denied
For the right one
A gift from the Gods
Or a cunning enemy
A force to be reckoned with
A beautiful giver of life
Or a natural disaster

Hello Self

Hello Self
I think it's time we reacquaint ourselves
I need you
Lost in the ever increasing negativity of
self-doubt
Spiraling into a darkness the longer you stay
A early contribute to an early grave
I need you to remember your fight
Come find me
I'm still within your reach
Grab and hold onto my embrace
Find your voice
Release the beast within you that will allow you
to be
Your light is brighter than the darkness
Your will is your life
I need you to fight for me
I beg of you self
Don't let me stay lost
I do want to live
Let's make our dreams bring forth to realities
that weren't meant to be pushed aside
Let's start again shall we
Look into a mirror deep down, find me and say
Hello Self

I received your message
We will rise again
We will live

Internal Burn

Outside I'm a calm and peaceful being
But inside a fire burns
Ready to explode and let loose
Only to be controlled an left to simmer
Waiting for the one to release it
Who will win in this ongoing battle for
domination

I am

I am a black woman
Smooth caramel mocha skin
Sweet
Addictive taste
To sample means to come back for more
Hypnotic
Sassy Look
With a stare
I draw you to me
Loyal
Honorable
Treat me right, I'll treat you right
I am a black woman
Nowhere near perfect
Lots of Flaws
Prideful I stand to hide behind a buffer for past
and future pains
Heartaches
I am a black woman
Here I stand with no discriminations against the
enemies of
Jealousy
Racism
No angel I be but No demon will take me

True to Me

Tempted by a possibility
Needing to release some untapped energy
I look to others and try to find strength within
them
I would like to find in myself
Never mistake me for weak
It's a decision I have made for myself
Never to let your voice bring me down
In that is where I stand strong
What makes me different than you
I'm not trying to understand me or you
I'm living in what's true to me
Not to say that it can't be changed
Because it can
Believe when a change is done
It wasn't because of you or your
Biased Opinions
It was because a decision was made by me
To make a choice to change
That will allow me to continue being
True To Me